Supplementary Material
for use with
JOHN THOMPSON'S MODERN COURSE FOR THE PIANO

FOURTH GRADE
ETUDES

Twenty-Four Progressive Studies in
all Major and Minor Keys from the
Works of Berens, Bertini, Cramer,
Czerny, Gurlitt, Heller, Leybach,
Löschhorn and John Thompson. Each
Containing Preparatory Exercises.

By

John Thompson

THE WILLIS MUSIC COMPANY

CONTENTS

In Progressive Succession

In the Order of Keys

FOREWORD

While this book is specially designed for supplementary use with the FOURTH GRADE BOOK in JOHN THOMPSON'S MODERN COURSE FOR THE PIANO, it will be found most practical for technical development in connection with any book of a similar grade.

Preparatory Exercises

Be sure to give full attention to the preparatory exercises preceding each étude. Not only will they simplify the mastery of the études themselves, but should teach the pupil how to make similar exercises of difficult passages occurring in solo pieces.

All Keys

To insure familiarity with all keys, études have been carefully selected requiring the pupil to play in twelve major and twelve minor keys.

A mastery of the contents of this book should provide a well-rounded technique and equip the pupil to play any material of Fourth Grade difficulty.

John Thompson

W. M. Co. 5930

Preparatory Exercises to No.1

JOHN THOMPSON

No.1

No. 2

No. 3

No. 1
Carl Czerny
(1791 - 1857)

Op. 718, No. 5

Preparatory Exercise to No. 2

Play the first section (first two lines) with FOREARM ATTACK.
The second (staccato) section may be played with either WRIST or FOREARM.

J. T.

No. 2
Cornelius Gurlitt
(1820 - 1901)

Adapted from Op. 50, No. 22

6

Preparatory Exercises to No. 3

J. T.

No. 1

Left Hand alone—Crisp staccato

No. 2

Strict Finger Legato

No. 3

Slowly with high finger action

W. M. Co. 5980-57

No. 3
Hermann Berens
(1825 - 1880)

Adapted from Op. 61, No. 13

Allegro risoluto

Preparatory Exercise to No. 4

J. T.

Allegretto scherzando

No. 4
Stephen Heller
(1813 -1888)

Practice the following exercise in two ways — using first WRIST STACCATO, then FINGER (plucking) STACCATO.

Op. 46, No. 2

Allegretto scherzando

Preparatory Exercises to No. 5

Use light, bouncing WRIST STACCATO.
Begin at slow tempo and develop speed *gradually*.

J. T.

No. 1

No. 2

No. 5
Henri (-Jerome) Bertini
(1798 - 1876)

Op. 29, No. 18

WRIST STACCATO

Preparatory Exercise to No. 6

FOREARM STACCATO

J. T.

No. 6
Albert Löschhorn
(1819 - 1905)

Practice also in G Minor

Op. 66, No. 8

Preparatory Exercise to No.7

No.1

J. T.

No. 2

No. 7
Henri Bertini
(1798 - 1876)

Op. 29, No. 5

Preparatory Exercise to No. 8

J. T.

No. 1

Moderato

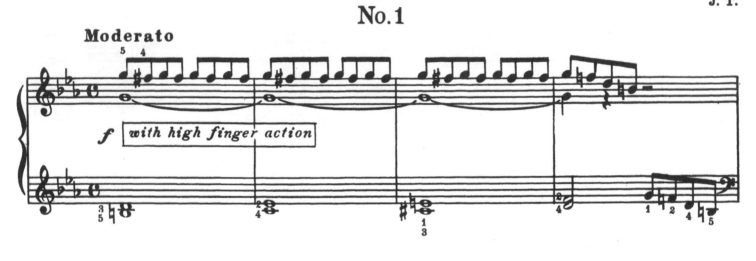

f with high finger action

No. 2

Allegro

No. 3

Allegro

No. 8
Stephen Heller
(1813 - 1888)

Op. 46, No. 5

Allegro

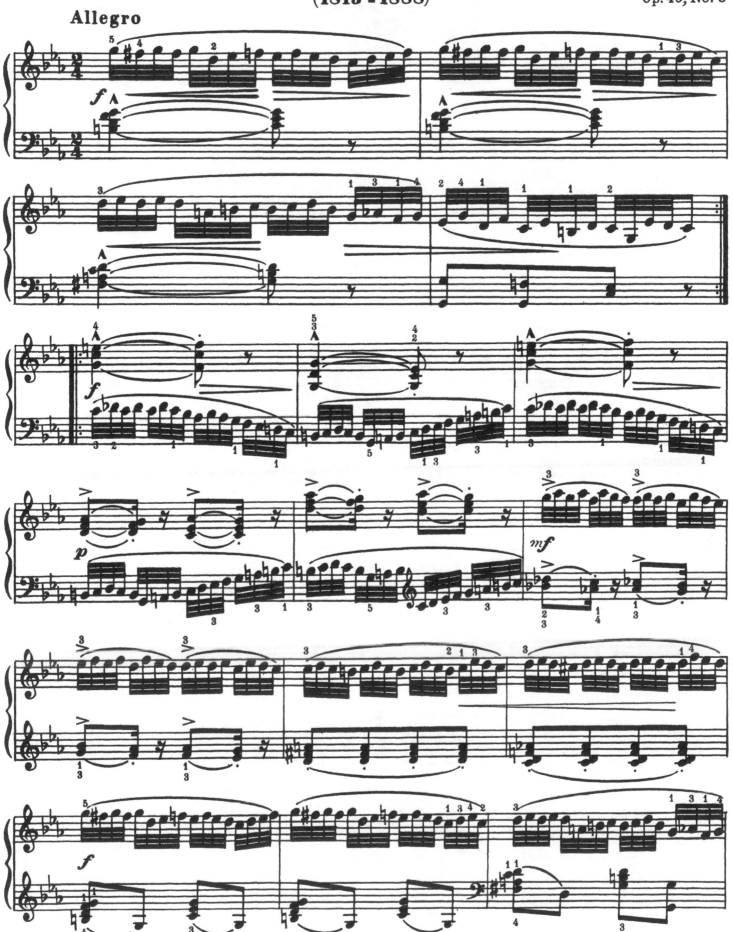

Preparatory Exercise to No. 9

J. T.

Allegretto

No. 9

JOHN THOMPSON

Preparatory Exercise to No. 10

J. T.

Andantino

No. 10
Stephen Heller
(1813-1888)

Op. 46, No. 11

Andantino

Preparatory Exercises to No. 11

No. 1

J. T.

No. 2

No. 11
Albert Löschhorn
(1819 - 1905)

Op. 66, No. 6

Preparatory Exercise to No.12

J. T.

Maestoso

No. 12
"Celestial Voices"

STEHEN HELLER, Op. 45, No. 9

Andante, quasi Allegretto

Note suggestion of "Adeste Fideles."

Preparatory Exercise to No. 13

No. 1

J. T.

No. 2

No. 13
Henri Bertini
(1798 - 1876)

Op. 29, No. 3

Preparatory Exercises to No. 14

No. 1

J.T.

No. 2

No. 14

JOHN THOMPSON

32

Preparatory Exercises to No.15

No.1

J.T.

Allegro

No.2

Allegro

W. M. Co. 5930-57

No. 15
Henri Bertini
(1798-1876)

Op. 29, No. 14

Allegro

Preparatory Exercise to No.16

Use **FOREARM PRESSURE TOUCH** with most of the weight resting on the upper notes of the right-hand chords— the melody tones.

Pedal may be used at the discretion of the teacher, in which case the pedal is changed on each chord.

Follow the phrasing marks exactly as indicated.

J. T.

Moderato

No. 16
Henri Bertini
(1798 - 1876)

Op. 29, No. 8

Allegretto

Preparatory Exercise to No. 17

J. T.

Moderato

Moderato

No. 17

JOHN THOMPSON

Preparatory Exercises to No. 18

J. T.

No. 1

No. 2

No. 18
Henri Bertini
(1798 - 1876)

Op. 29, No. 20

Preparatory Exercise to No. 19

J. T.

No. 19
John Baptiste Cramer
(1771 - 1858)

Arranged from the famous **50** Selected Studies gathered together by von Bülow from the 5th part of Cramer's "Practical Piano School."

Preparatory Exercise to No. 20

J. T.

No. 20
Carl Czerny
(1791 - 1857)

Op. 299, No. 13

Preparatory Exercise to No. 21

J. T.

Allegretto

No. 21

JOHN THOMPSON

Preparatory Exercise to No. 22

J. T.

No. 22

JOHN THOMPSON

Preparatory Exercise to No. 23

from
Löschhorn Op. 22

Combined wrist and
forearm staccato.
Be sure to observe
all repeat signs.

No. 23
from
La Diabolique

LEYBACH

Presto

p

sempre staccato

senza pedale

cres - - cen - - do

cres - cen - do

p

54

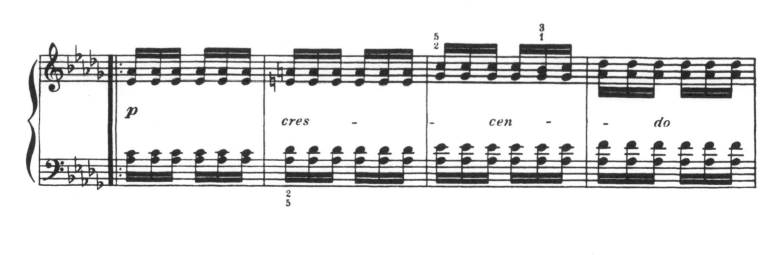

Preparatory Exercise to No. 24

J. T.

No. 24
Left Hand Alone

JOHN THOMPSON